Jan Feb Mar Apr May Jun Jul

1 2 3 4 5 6 7 8 9 10 11 12 13 14 15 16

26 27 28 29 30 31

MW01440543

Description:

"Can You Rock a Paper Bag? Fashion Wellness Journal" is a guided journal that embraces the concept of fashion wellness, focusing on feeling good before you put on your clothes. This unique journal combines self-love prompts, style and fashion wellness prompts, confidence boosters, and exercises to help you cultivate a sense of worthiness. It encourages you to explore your personal style, embrace self-expression, and build confidence from within. Through thought-provoking prompts and insightful reflections, you will discover how to rock any outfit with confidence and recognize your inherent worth. This journal is the first installment in the Can You Rock a Paper Bag - Fashion Wellness series, encompassing all aspects of self-love, style, and empowerment.

Write down three things that you appreciate about yourself, and why they're important to you.

Take some time to think about your strengths, qualities, and values. What do you like about yourself?

What are you proud of? These can be big or small things - from your sense of humor to your ability to listen to others.

Jan Feb Mar Apr May Jun Jul Aug Sept Oct Nov Dec

1 2 3 4 5 6 7 8 9 10 11 12 13 14 15 16 17 18 19 20 21 22 23 24 25 26 27 28 29 30 31

Think about a time when you felt really confident and empowered. What was it about that experience that made you feel that way? How can you cultivate that feeling more often? Reflect on times when you've felt confident and empowered - whether it's when you're speaking up for yourself, accomplishing a goal, or simply feeling comfortable in your own skin.

Jan Feb Mar Apr May Jun Jul Aug Sept Oct Nov Dec

1 2 3 4 5 6 7 8 9 10 11 12 13 14 15 16 17 18 19 20 21 22 23 24 25 26 27 28 29 30 31

What are some negative self-talk patterns that you tend to engage in? How can you challenge and reframe those thoughts?

We all have a critical voice in our heads at times, but sometimes that voice can become overly negative and harsh.Think about the negative self-talk patterns that you tend to engage in. What do you say to yourself when you're feeling down or insecure?

Jan Feb Mar Apr May Jun Jul Aug Sept Oct Nov Dec

1 2 3 4 5 6 7 8 9 10 11 12 13 14 15 16 17 18 19 20 21 22 23 24 25 26 27 28 29 30 31

How can you challenge those thoughts and reframe them in a more positive, compassionate way?

What are your biggest fears or insecurities? How can you show yourself compassion and love when these fears or insecurities come up? We all have fears and insecurities, but it's important to acknowledge and address them rather than trying to ignore or suppress them. Think about your biggest fears or insecurities. How do they make you feel? How can you show yourself compassion and love when these feelings come up? What strategies can you use to work through them?

Jan Feb Mar Apr May Jun Jul Aug Sept Oct Nov Dec

1 2 3 4 5 6 7 8 9 10 11 12 13 14 15 16 17 18 19 20 21 22 23 24 25 26 27 28 29 30 31

Self-care and self-love are important practices that help us to feel more balanced and fulfilled in our lives. Think about some ways that you can practice self-care and self-love on a daily basis.What are some ways that you can practice self-care and self-love on a daily basis? This

Jan Feb Mar Apr May Jun Jul Aug Sept Oct Nov Dec

1 2 3 4 5 6 7 8 9 10 11 12 13 14 15 16 17 18 19 20 21 22 23 24 25
26 27 28 29 30 31

could include things like getting enough sleep, eating nourishing foods, spending time in nature, connecting with loved ones, or doing activities that bring you joy.

Jan Feb Mar Apr May Jun Jul Aug Sept Oct Nov Dec

1 2 3 4 5 6 7 8 9 10 11 12 13 14 15 16 17 18 19 20 21 22 23 24 25 26 27 28 29 30 31

Many of us have dreams or goals that we've been wanting to pursue but haven't yet taken the steps to make them a reality.

What is something that you've been wanting to do but have been holding yourself back from?

How can you give yourself permission to pursue that thing?

Think about something that you've been wanting to do but have been holding yourself back from. What's been holding you back?

How can you give yourself permission to pursue that thing - whether it's through taking small steps or seeking support from others?

Jan Feb Mar Apr May Jun Jul Aug Sept Oct Nov Dec

1 2 3 4 5 6 7 8 9 10 11 12 13 14 15 16 17 18 19 20 21 22 23 24 25 26 27 28 29 30 31

Think of a time when you overcame a challenge or obstacle. What strengths or qualities did you draw on to get through that experience?

We all face challenges and obstacles in our lives, but it's important to remember the times when we've overcome them. Think about a time when you faced a challenge or obstacle and were able to overcome it. What strengths or qualities did you draw on to get through that experience? How can you apply those strengths and qualities to other areas of your life?

Jan Feb Mar Apr May Jun Jul Aug Sept Oct Nov Dec

1 2 3 4 5 6 7 8 9 10 11 12 13 14 15 16 17 18 19 20 21 22 23 24 25 26 27 28 29 30 31

Many of us have limiting beliefs about ourselves that hold us back from achieving our full potential. Think about some of the limiting beliefs that you have about yourself - whether it's that you're not good enough, not smart enough, or not capable enough. How can you start to shift those beliefs to be more empowering and supportive of your growth and development?

Jan Feb Mar Apr May Jun Jul Aug Sept Oct Nov Dec

1 2 3 4 5 6 7 8 9 10 11 12 13 14 15 16 17 18 19 20 21 22 23 24 25 26 27 28 29 30 31

What are some limiting beliefs that you have about yourself? How can you start to shift those beliefs to be more empowering?

What is one thing that you can do today to show yourself love and kindness?

Jan Feb Mar Apr May Jun Jul Aug Sept Oct Nov Dec

1 2 3 4 5 6 7 8 9 10 11 12 13 14 15 16 17 18 19 20 21 22 23 24 25
26 27 28 29 30 31

Jan Feb Mar Apr May Jun Jul Aug Sept Oct Nov Dec

1 2 3 4 5 6 7 8 9 10 11 12 13 14 15 16 17 18 19 20 21 22 23 24 25 26 27 28 29 30 31

Jan Feb Mar Apr May Jun Jul Aug Sept Oct Nov Dec

1 2 3 4 5 6 7 8 9 10 11 12 13 14 15 16 17 18 19 20 21 22 23 24 25 26 27 28 29 30 31

Jan Feb Mar Apr May Jun Jul Aug Sept Oct Nov Dec

1 2 3 4 5 6 7 8 9 10 11 12 13 14 15 16 17 18 19 20 21 22 23 24 25 26 27 28 29 30 31

Jan Feb Mar Apr May Jun Jul Aug Sept Oct Nov Dec

1 2 3 4 5 6 7 8 9 10 11 12 13 14 15 16 17 18 19 20 21 22 23 24 25
26 27 28 29 30 31

Jan Feb Mar Apr May Jun Jul Aug Sept Oct Nov Dec

1 2 3 4 5 6 7 8 9 10 11 12 13 14 15 16 17 18 19 20 21 22 23 24 25 26 27 28 29 30 31

Jan Feb Mar Apr May Jun Jul Aug Sept Oct Nov Dec

1 2 3 4 5 6 7 8 9 10 11 12 13 14 15 16 17 18 19 20 21 22 23 24 25

26 27 28 29 30 31

Jan Feb Mar Apr May Jun Jul Aug Sept Oct Nov Dec

1 2 3 4 5 6 7 8 9 10 11 12 13 14 15 16 17 18 19 20 21 22 23 24 25
26 27 28 29 30 31

Jan Feb Mar Apr May Jun Jul Aug Sept Oct Nov Dec

1 2 3 4 5 6 7 8 9 10 11 12 13 14 15 16 17 18 19 20 21 22 23 24 25 26 27 28 29 30 31

Jan Feb Mar Apr May Jun Jul Aug Sept Oct Nov Dec

1 2 3 4 5 6 7 8 9 10 11 12 13 14 15 16 17 18 19 20 21 22 23 24 25

26 27 28 29 30 31

Jan Feb Mar Apr May Jun Jul Aug Sept Oct Nov Dec

1 2 3 4 5 6 7 8 9 10 11 12 13 14 15 16 17 18 19 20 21 22 23 24 25 26 27 28 29 30 31

Jan Feb Mar Apr May Jun Jul Aug Sept Oct Nov Dec

1 2 3 4 5 6 7 8 9 10 11 12 13 14 15 16 17 18 19 20 21 22 23 24 25

26 27 28 29 30 31

Jan Feb Mar Apr May Jun Jul Aug Sept Oct Nov Dec

1 2 3 4 5 6 7 8 9 10 11 12 13 14 15 16 17 18 19 20 21 22 23 24 25 26 27 28 29 30 31

Jan Feb Mar Apr May Jun Jul Aug Sept Oct Nov Dec

1 2 3 4 5 6 7 8 9 10 11 12 13 14 15 16 17 18 19 20 21 22 23 24 25

26 27 28 29 30 31

Jan Feb Mar Apr May Jun Jul Aug Sept Oct Nov Dec

1 2 3 4 5 6 7 8 9 10 11 12 13 14 15 16 17 18 19 20 21 22 23 24 25
26 27 28 29 30 31

Jan Feb Mar Apr May Jun Jul Aug Sept Oct Nov Dec

1 2 3 4 5 6 7 8 9 10 11 12 13 14 15 16 17 18 19 20 21 22 23 24 25
26 27 28 29 30 31

Jan Feb Mar Apr May Jun Jul Aug Sept Oct Nov Dec

1 2 3 4 5 6 7 8 9 10 11 12 13 14 15 16 17 18 19 20 21 22 23 24 25 26 27 28 29 30 31

Jan Feb Mar Apr May Jun Jul Aug Sept Oct Nov Dec

1 2 3 4 5 6 7 8 9 10 11 12 13 14 15 16 17 18 19 20 21 22 23 24 25

26 27 28 29 30 31

Jan Feb Mar Apr May Jun Jul Aug Sept Oct Nov Dec

1 2 3 4 5 6 7 8 9 10 11 12 13 14 15 16 17 18 19 20 21 22 23 24 25 26 27 28 29 30 31

Jan Feb Mar Apr May Jun Jul Aug Sept Oct Nov Dec

1 2 3 4 5 6 7 8 9 10 11 12 13 14 15 16 17 18 19 20 21 22 23 24 25

26 27 28 29 30 31

Jan Feb Mar Apr May Jun Jul Aug Sept Oct Nov Dec

1 2 3 4 5 6 7 8 9 10 11 12 13 14 15 16 17 18 19 20 21 22 23 24 25
26 27 28 29 30 31

Jan Feb Mar Apr May Jun Jul Aug Sept Oct Nov Dec

1 2 3 4 5 6 7 8 9 10 11 12 13 14 15 16 17 18 19 20 21 22 23 24 25 26 27 28 29 30 31

Jan Feb Mar Apr May Jun Jul Aug Sept Oct Nov Dec

1 2 3 4 5 6 7 8 9 10 11 12 13 14 15 16 17 18 19 20 21 22 23 24 25 26 27 28 29 30 31

Jan Feb Mar Apr May Jun Jul Aug Sept Oct Nov Dec

1 2 3 4 5 6 7 8 9 10 11 12 13 14 15 16 17 18 19 20 21 22 23 24 25 26 27 28 29 30 31

Jan Feb Mar Apr May Jun Jul Aug Sept Oct Nov Dec

1 2 3 4 5 6 7 8 9 10 11 12 13 14 15 16 17 18 19 20 21 22 23 24 25 26 27 28 29 30 31

Before you get dressed, take some time to connect with your body. Close your eyes and take a few deep breaths, focusing on the sensation of your breath moving in and out of your body. Then, scan your body from head to toe, noticing any sensations or feelings that come up. Take note of any areas that feel tense or uncomfortable, and see if you can release any tension or discomfort through gentle movements or stretches.

Jan Feb Mar Apr May Jun Jul Aug Sept Oct Nov Dec

1 2 3 4 5 6 7 8 9 10 11 12 13 14 15 16 17 18 19 20 21 22 23 24 25 26 27 28 29 30 31

Think about what clothes make you feel most confident and comfortable, and write down why. Is it how they fit your body, or how they hug your curves, perhaps how they feel on your skin.

Jan Feb Mar Apr May Jun Jul Aug Sept Oct Nov Dec

1 2 3 4 5 6 7 8 9 10 11 12 13 14 15 16 17 18 19 20 21 22 23 24 25 26 27 28 29 30 31

What colors, fabrics, and styles do you love? Take some time to explore your personal style and preferences. Consider creating a mood board or Pinterest board of outfits that inspire you and make you feel good.

Jan Feb Mar Apr May Jun Jul Aug Sept Oct Nov Dec

1 2 3 4 5 6 7 8 9 10 11 12 13 14 15 16 17 18 19 20 21 22 23 24 25 26 27 28 29 30 31

Write down three things that you love about your body, and why. This could be anything from your strong legs to your sparkling eyes. Focus on the things that you appreciate about your body, rather than the things you want to change.

Jan Feb Mar Apr May Jun Jul Aug Sept Oct Nov Dec

1 2 3 4 5 6 7 8 9 10 11 12 13 14 15 16 17 18 19 20 21 22 23 24 25 26 27 28 29 30 31

Now write down three things that you hate about your body, and why.

Those thing you wrote down that you hate, I need you to write them down again, and read them out loud, . For ecamples, I hate my eyes, I own it, because their mines, and I love them because I love me.

Jan Feb Mar Apr May Jun Jul Aug Sept Oct Nov Dec

1 2 3 4 5 6 7 8 9 10 11 12 13 14 15 16 17 18 19 20 21 22 23 24 25 26 27 28 29 30 31

Set an intention for how you want to feel in your clothes today. Do you want to feel comfortable, confident, powerful, or playful? Whatever it is, set an intention for how you want to feel in your clothes and choose an outfit that supports that intention.

Jan Feb Mar Apr May Jun Jul Aug Sept Oct Nov Dec

1 2 3 4 5 6 7 8 9 10 11 12 13 14 15 16 17 18 19 20 21 22 23 24 25 26 27 28 29 30 31

Practice gratitude for your clothes and accessories. Take a moment to appreciate the clothes and accessories that you have and the role that they play in your life. Think about the stories behind your favorite pieces and the memories that you associate with them. Because every outfit has a story, what your outfit story, of what you have on today?

Jan Feb Mar Apr May Jun Jul Aug Sept Oct Nov Dec

1 2 3 4 5 6 7 8 9 10 11 12 13 14 15 16 17 18 19 20 21 22 23 24 25 26 27 28 29 30 31

Todays outfits story is:

Practice self-compassion if you're having a "bad outfit day." And what made that outfit bad? We all have days when we don't feel great in our clothes, and that's okay. Practice self-compassion and remind yourself that your worth and value are not determined by how you look. Take some deep breaths, do something that makes you feel good, and try again tomorrow.

Jan Feb Mar Apr May Jun Jul Aug Sept Oct Nov Dec

1 2 3 4 5 6 7 8 9 10 11 12 13 14 15 16 17 18 19 20 21 22 23 24 25 26 27 28 29 30 31

Jan Feb Mar Apr May Jun Jul Aug Sept Oct Nov Dec

1 2 3 4 5 6 7 8 9 10 11 12 13 14 15 16 17 18 19 20 21 22 23 24 25 26 27 28 29 30 31

Jan Feb Mar Apr May Jun Jul Aug Sept Oct Nov Dec

1 2 3 4 5 6 7 8 9 10 11 12 13 14 15 16 17 18 19 20 21 22 23 24 25
26 27 28 29 30 31

Jan Feb Mar Apr May Jun Jul Aug Sept Oct Nov Dec

1 2 3 4 5 6 7 8 9 10 11 12 13 14 15 16 17 18 19 20 21 22 23 24 25
26 27 28 29 30 31

Jan Feb Mar Apr May Jun Jul Aug Sept Oct Nov Dec

1 2 3 4 5 6 7 8 9 10 11 12 13 14 15 16 17 18 19 20 21 22 23 24 25
26 27 28 29 30 31

Jan Feb Mar Apr May Jun Jul Aug Sept Oct Nov Dec

1 2 3 4 5 6 7 8 9 10 11 12 13 14 15 16 17 18 19 20 21 22 23 24 25 26 27 28 29 30 31

Jan Feb Mar Apr May Jun Jul Aug Sept Oct Nov Dec

1 2 3 4 5 6 7 8 9 10 11 12 13 14 15 16 17 18 19 20 21 22 23 24 25 26 27 28 29 30 31

Jan Feb Mar Apr May Jun Jul Aug Sept Oct Nov Dec

1 2 3 4 5 6 7 8 9 10 11 12 13 14 15 16 17 18 19 20 21 22 23 24 25 26 27 28 29 30 31

Jan Feb Mar Apr May Jun Jul Aug Sept Oct Nov Dec

1 2 3 4 5 6 7 8 9 10 11 12 13 14 15 16 17 18 19 20 21 22 23 24 25 26 27 28 29 30 31

Jan Feb Mar Apr May Jun Jul Aug Sept Oct Nov Dec

1 2 3 4 5 6 7 8 9 10 11 12 13 14 15 16 17 18 19 20 21 22 23 24 25
26 27 28 29 30 31

Jan Feb Mar Apr May Jun Jul Aug Sept Oct Nov Dec

1 2 3 4 5 6 7 8 9 10 11 12 13 14 15 16 17 18 19 20 21 22 23 24 25 26 27 28 29 30 31

Jan Feb Mar Apr May Jun Jul Aug Sept Oct Nov Dec

1 2 3 4 5 6 7 8 9 10 11 12 13 14 15 16 17 18 19 20 21 22 23 24 25

26 27 28 29 30 31

Jan Feb Mar Apr May Jun Jul Aug Sept Oct Nov Dec

1 2 3 4 5 6 7 8 9 10 11 12 13 14 15 16 17 18 19 20 21 22 23 24 25
26 27 28 29 30 31

Jan Feb Mar Apr May Jun Jul Aug Sept Oct Nov Dec

1 2 3 4 5 6 7 8 9 10 11 12 13 14 15 16 17 18 19 20 21 22 23 24 25 26 27 28 29 30 31

Jan Feb Mar Apr May Jun Jul Aug Sept Oct Nov Dec

1 2 3 4 5 6 7 8 9 10 11 12 13 14 15 16 17 18 19 20 21 22 23 24 25
26 27 28 29 30 31

Jan Feb Mar Apr May Jun Jul Aug Sept Oct Nov Dec

1 2 3 4 5 6 7 8 9 10 11 12 13 14 15 16 17 18 19 20 21 22 23 24 25
26 27 28 29 30 31

Jan Feb Mar Apr May Jun Jul Aug Sept Oct Nov Dec

1 2 3 4 5 6 7 8 9 10 11 12 13 14 15 16 17 18 19 20 21 22 23 24 25 26 27 28 29 30 31

Jan Feb Mar Apr May Jun Jul Aug Sept Oct Nov Dec

1 2 3 4 5 6 7 8 9 10 11 12 13 14 15 16 17 18 19 20 21 22 23 24 25

26 27 28 29 30 31

Jan Feb Mar Apr May Jun Jul Aug Sept Oct Nov Dec

1 2 3 4 5 6 7 8 9 10 11 12 13 14 15 16 17 18 19 20 21 22 23 24 25
26 27 28 29 30 31

Jan Feb Mar Apr May Jun Jul Aug Sept Oct Nov Dec

1 2 3 4 5 6 7 8 9 10 11 12 13 14 15 16 17 18 19 20 21 22 23 24 25 26 27 28 29 30 31

Jan Feb Mar Apr May Jun Jul Aug Sept Oct Nov Dec

1 2 3 4 5 6 7 8 9 10 11 12 13 14 15 16 17 18 19 20 21 22 23 24 25
26 27 28 29 30 31

Jan Feb Mar Apr May Jun Jul Aug Sept Oct Nov Dec

1 2 3 4 5 6 7 8 9 10 11 12 13 14 15 16 17 18 19 20 21 22 23 24 25 26 27 28 29 30 31

Jan Feb Mar Apr May Jun Jul Aug Sept Oct Nov Dec

1 2 3 4 5 6 7 8 9 10 11 12 13 14 15 16 17 18 19 20 21 22 23 24 25

26 27 28 29 30 31

Jan Feb Mar Apr May Jun Jul Aug Sept Oct Nov Dec

1 2 3 4 5 6 7 8 9 10 11 12 13 14 15 16 17 18 19 20 21 22 23 24 25 26 27 28 29 30 31

Jan Feb Mar Apr May Jun Jul Aug Sept Oct Nov Dec

1 2 3 4 5 6 7 8 9 10 11 12 13 14 15 16 17 18 19 20 21 22 23 24 25
26 27 28 29 30 31

Jan Feb Mar Apr May Jun Jul Aug Sept Oct Nov Dec

1 2 3 4 5 6 7 8 9 10 11 12 13 14 15 16 17 18 19 20 21 22 23 24 25
26 27 28 29 30 31

Jan Feb Mar Apr May Jun Jul Aug Sept Oct Nov Dec

1 2 3 4 5 6 7 8 9 10 11 12 13 14 15 16 17 18 19 20 21 22 23 24 25

26 27 28 29 30 31

Jan Feb Mar Apr May Jun Jul Aug Sept Oct Nov Dec

1 2 3 4 5 6 7 8 9 10 11 12 13 14 15 16 17 18 19 20 21 22 23 24 25 26 27 28 29 30 31

Jan Feb Mar Apr May Jun Jul Aug Sept Oct Nov Dec

1 2 3 4 5 6 7 8 9 10 11 12 13 14 15 16 17 18 19 20 21 22 23 24 25 26 27 28 29 30 31

Jan Feb Mar Apr May Jun Jul Aug Sept Oct Nov Dec

1 2 3 4 5 6 7 8 9 10 11 12 13 14 15 16 17 18 19 20 21 22 23 24 25 26 27 28 29 30 31

Jan Feb Mar Apr May Jun Jul Aug Sept Oct Nov Dec

1 2 3 4 5 6 7 8 9 10 11 12 13 14 15 16 17 18 19 20 21 22 23 24 25
26 27 28 29 30 31

Jan Feb Mar Apr May Jun Jul Aug Sept Oct Nov Dec

1 2 3 4 5 6 7 8 9 10 11 12 13 14 15 16 17 18 19 20 21 22 23 24 25
26 27 28 29 30 31

Jan Feb Mar Apr May Jun Jul Aug Sept Oct Nov Dec

1 2 3 4 5 6 7 8 9 10 11 12 13 14 15 16 17 18 19 20 21 22 23 24 25 26 27 28 29 30 31

Jan Feb Mar Apr May Jun Jul Aug Sept Oct Nov Dec

1 2 3 4 5 6 7 8 9 10 11 12 13 14 15 16 17 18 19 20 21 22 23 24 25 26 27 28 29 30 31

Jan Feb Mar Apr May Jun Jul Aug Sept Oct Nov Dec

1 2 3 4 5 6 7 8 9 10 11 12 13 14 15 16 17 18 19 20 21 22 23 24 25

26 27 28 29 30 31

Jan Feb Mar Apr May Jun Jul Aug Sept Oct Nov Dec

1 2 3 4 5 6 7 8 9 10 11 12 13 14 15 16 17 18 19 20 21 22 23 24 25 26 27 28 29 30 31

Jan Feb Mar Apr May Jun Jul Aug Sept Oct Nov Dec

1 2 3 4 5 6 7 8 9 10 11 12 13 14 15 16 17 18 19 20 21 22 23 24 25
26 27 28 29 30 31

Jan Feb Mar Apr May Jun Jul Aug Sept Oct Nov Dec

1 2 3 4 5 6 7 8 9 10 11 12 13 14 15 16 17 18 19 20 21 22 23 24 25 26 27 28 29 30 31

Jan Feb Mar Apr May Jun Jul Aug Sept Oct Nov Dec

1 2 3 4 5 6 7 8 9 10 11 12 13 14 15 16 17 18 19 20 21 22 23 24 25 26 27 28 29 30 31

Jan Feb Mar Apr May Jun Jul Aug Sept Oct Nov Dec

1 2 3 4 5 6 7 8 9 10 11 12 13 14 15 16 17 18 19 20 21 22 23 24 25
26 27 28 29 30 31

Jan Feb Mar Apr May Jun Jul Aug Sept Oct Nov Dec

1 2 3 4 5 6 7 8 9 10 11 12 13 14 15 16 17 18 19 20 21 22 23 24 25 26 27 28 29 30 31

Jan Feb Mar Apr May Jun Jul Aug Sept Oct Nov Dec

1 2 3 4 5 6 7 8 9 10 11 12 13 14 15 16 17 18 19 20 21 22 23 24 25 26 27 28 29 30 31

Jan Feb Mar Apr May Jun Jul Aug Sept Oct Nov Dec

1 2 3 4 5 6 7 8 9 10 11 12 13 14 15 16 17 18 19 20 21 22 23 24 25
26 27 28 29 30 31

Jan Feb Mar Apr May Jun Jul Aug Sept Oct Nov Dec

1 2 3 4 5 6 7 8 9 10 11 12 13 14 15 16 17 18 19 20 21 22 23 24 25
26 27 28 29 30 31

Jan Feb Mar Apr May Jun Jul Aug Sept Oct Nov Dec

1 2 3 4 5 6 7 8 9 10 11 12 13 14 15 16 17 18 19 20 21 22 23 24 25 26 27 28 29 30 31

Jan Feb Mar Apr May Jun Jul Aug Sept Oct Nov Dec

1 2 3 4 5 6 7 8 9 10 11 12 13 14 15 16 17 18 19 20 21 22 23 24 25
26 27 28 29 30 31

Jan Feb Mar Apr May Jun Jul Aug Sept Oct Nov Dec

1 2 3 4 5 6 7 8 9 10 11 12 13 14 15 16 17 18 19 20 21 22 23 24 25 26 27 28 29 30 31

Jan Feb Mar Apr May Jun Jul Aug Sept Oct Nov Dec

1 2 3 4 5 6 7 8 9 10 11 12 13 14 15 16 17 18 19 20 21 22 23 24 25
26 27 28 29 30 31

Jan Feb Mar Apr May Jun Jul Aug Sept Oct Nov Dec

1 2 3 4 5 6 7 8 9 10 11 12 13 14 15 16 17 18 19 20 21 22 23 24 25

26 27 28 29 30 31

Jan Feb Mar Apr May Jun Jul Aug Sept Oct Nov Dec

1 2 3 4 5 6 7 8 9 10 11 12 13 14 15 16 17 18 19 20 21 22 23 24 25 26 27 28 29 30 31

Jan Feb Mar Apr May Jun Jul Aug Sept Oct Nov Dec

1 2 3 4 5 6 7 8 9 10 11 12 13 14 15 16 17 18 19 20 21 22 23 24 25
26 27 28 29 30 31

Jan Feb Mar Apr May Jun Jul Aug Sept Oct Nov Dec

1 2 3 4 5 6 7 8 9 10 11 12 13 14 15 16 17 18 19 20 21 22 23 24 25
26 27 28 29 30 31

Jan Feb Mar Apr May Jun Jul Aug Sept Oct Nov Dec

1 2 3 4 5 6 7 8 9 10 11 12 13 14 15 16 17 18 19 20 21 22 23 24 25
26 27 28 29 30 31

Jan Feb Mar Apr May Jun Jul Aug Sept Oct Nov Dec

1 2 3 4 5 6 7 8 9 10 11 12 13 14 15 16 17 18 19 20 21 22 23 24 25
26 27 28 29 30 31

Jan Feb Mar Apr May Jun Jul Aug Sept Oct Nov Dec

1 2 3 4 5 6 7 8 9 10 11 12 13 14 15 16 17 18 19 20 21 22 23 24 25
26 27 28 29 30 31

Jan Feb Mar Apr May Jun Jul Aug Sept Oct Nov Dec

1 2 3 4 5 6 7 8 9 10 11 12 13 14 15 16 17 18 19 20 21 22 23 24 25

26 27 28 29 30 31

Jan Feb Mar Apr May Jun Jul Aug Sept Oct Nov Dec

1 2 3 4 5 6 7 8 9 10 11 12 13 14 15 16 17 18 19 20 21 22 23 24 25
26 27 28 29 30 31

Jan Feb Mar Apr May Jun Jul Aug Sept Oct Nov Dec

1 2 3 4 5 6 7 8 9 10 11 12 13 14 15 16 17 18 19 20 21 22 23 24 25

26 27 28 29 30 31

Jan Feb Mar Apr May Jun Jul Aug Sept Oct Nov Dec

1 2 3 4 5 6 7 8 9 10 11 12 13 14 15 16 17 18 19 20 21 22 23 24 25

26 27 28 29 30 31

Jan Feb Mar Apr May Jun Jul Aug Sept Oct Nov Dec

1 2 3 4 5 6 7 8 9 10 11 12 13 14 15 16 17 18 19 20 21 22 23 24 25 26 27 28 29 30 31

Jan Feb Mar Apr May Jun Jul Aug Sept Oct Nov Dec

1 2 3 4 5 6 7 8 9 10 11 12 13 14 15 16 17 18 19 20 21 22 23 24 25
26 27 28 29 30 31

Jan Feb Mar Apr May Jun Jul Aug Sept Oct Nov Dec

1 2 3 4 5 6 7 8 9 10 11 12 13 14 15 16 17 18 19 20 21 22 23 24 25 26 27 28 29 30 31

Jan Feb Mar Apr May Jun Jul Aug Sept Oct Nov Dec

1 2 3 4 5 6 7 8 9 10 11 12 13 14 15 16 17 18 19 20 21 22 23 24 25
26 27 28 29 30 31

Jan Feb Mar Apr May Jun Jul Aug Sept Oct Nov Dec

1 2 3 4 5 6 7 8 9 10 11 12 13 14 15 16 17 18 19 20 21 22 23 24 25 26 27 28 29 30 31

Confidence is a state of mind characterized by a belief in one's abilities, worth, and potential for success. It is an inner sense of self-assurance and belief in one's own judgments and decisions. Having confidence means having faith in yourself and your capabilities, and it plays a significant role in shaping your life in several ways.

Think about a time when you felt confident and empowered. What were you doing? Who were you with? What thoughts and feelings were running through your mind? Write down this experience in detail, and use it as a reference point for how you want to feel in the future.

Jan Feb Mar Apr May Jun Jul Aug Sept Oct Nov Dec

1 2 3 4 5 6 7 8 9 10 11 12 13 14 15 16 17 18 19 20 21 22 23 24 25
26 27 28 29 30 31

Set achievable goals for yourself. Think about something you've been wanting to do but haven't yet, and break it down into smaller, manageable steps. Write down these steps and commit to taking action on them. Celebrate each step you take towards achieving your goal, and acknowledge the progress you've made. What are some goals you want to achieve.

Jan Feb Mar Apr May Jun Jul Aug Sept Oct Nov Dec

1 2 3 4 5 6 7 8 9 10 11 12 13 14 15 16 17 18 19 20 21 22 23 24 25 26 27 28 29 30 31

Practice self-care. Take time to care for yourself physically, mentally, and emotionally. This could be anything from taking a relaxing bath to practicing yoga to talking with a therapist. Prioritize your own well-being, and recognize that self-care is an essential component of building confidence and resilience.

What are some self-care things you could start doing today? Make a list 3 for each category, physical, mental, and emotional.

Jan Feb Mar Apr May Jun Jul Aug Sept Oct Nov Dec

1 2 3 4 5 6 7 8 9 10 11 12 13 14 15 16 17 18 19 20 21 22 23 24 25

26 27 28 29 30 31

Jan Feb Mar Apr May Jun Jul Aug Sept Oct Nov Dec

1 2 3 4 5 6 7 8 9 10 11 12 13 14 15 16 17 18 19 20 21 22 23 24 25 26 27 28 29 30 31

Jan Feb Mar Apr May Jun Jul Aug Sept Oct Nov Dec

1 2 3 4 5 6 7 8 9 10 11 12 13 14 15 16 17 18 19 20 21 22 23 24 25

26 27 28 29 30 31

Jan Feb Mar Apr May Jun Jul Aug Sept Oct Nov Dec

1 2 3 4 5 6 7 8 9 10 11 12 13 14 15 16 17 18 19 20 21 22 23 24 25
26 27 28 29 30 31

Jan Feb Mar Apr May Jun Jul Aug Sept Oct Nov Dec

1 2 3 4 5 6 7 8 9 10 11 12 13 14 15 16 17 18 19 20 21 22 23 24 25 26 27 28 29 30 31

Jan Feb Mar Apr May Jun Jul Aug Sept Oct Nov Dec

1 2 3 4 5 6 7 8 9 10 11 12 13 14 15 16 17 18 19 20 21 22 23 24 25 26 27 28 29 30 31

Jan Feb Mar Apr May Jun Jul Aug Sept Oct Nov Dec

1 2 3 4 5 6 7 8 9 10 11 12 13 14 15 16 17 18 19 20 21 22 23 24 25
26 27 28 29 30 31

Jan Feb Mar Apr May Jun Jul Aug Sept Oct Nov Dec

1 2 3 4 5 6 7 8 9 10 11 12 13 14 15 16 17 18 19 20 21 22 23 24 25

26 27 28 29 30 31

Jan Feb Mar Apr May Jun Jul Aug Sept Oct Nov Dec

1 2 3 4 5 6 7 8 9 10 11 12 13 14 15 16 17 18 19 20 21 22 23 24 25 26 27 28 29 30 31

Jan Feb Mar Apr May Jun Jul Aug Sept Oct Nov Dec

1 2 3 4 5 6 7 8 9 10 11 12 13 14 15 16 17 18 19 20 21 22 23 24 25

26 27 28 29 30 31

Jan Feb Mar Apr May Jun Jul Aug Sept Oct Nov Dec

1 2 3 4 5 6 7 8 9 10 11 12 13 14 15 16 17 18 19 20 21 22 23 24 25 26 27 28 29 30 31

Jan Feb Mar Apr May Jun Jul Aug Sept Oct Nov Dec

1 2 3 4 5 6 7 8 9 10 11 12 13 14 15 16 17 18 19 20 21 22 23 24 25 26 27 28 29 30 31

Jan Feb Mar Apr May Jun Jul Aug Sept Oct Nov Dec

1 2 3 4 5 6 7 8 9 10 11 12 13 14 15 16 17 18 19 20 21 22 23 24 25
26 27 28 29 30 31

Jan Feb Mar Apr May Jun Jul Aug Sept Oct Nov Dec

1 2 3 4 5 6 7 8 9 10 11 12 13 14 15 16 17 18 19 20 21 22 23 24 25

26 27 28 29 30 31

Jan Feb Mar Apr May Jun Jul Aug Sept Oct Nov Dec

1 2 3 4 5 6 7 8 9 10 11 12 13 14 15 16 17 18 19 20 21 22 23 24 25
26 27 28 29 30 31

Jan Feb Mar Apr May Jun Jul Aug Sept Oct Nov Dec

1 2 3 4 5 6 7 8 9 10 11 12 13 14 15 16 17 18 19 20 21 22 23 24 25

26 27 28 29 30 31

Jan Feb Mar Apr May Jun Jul Aug Sept Oct Nov Dec

1 2 3 4 5 6 7 8 9 10 11 12 13 14 15 16 17 18 19 20 21 22 23 24 25

26 27 28 29 30 31

Jan Feb Mar Apr May Jun Jul Aug Sept Oct Nov Dec

1 2 3 4 5 6 7 8 9 10 11 12 13 14 15 16 17 18 19 20 21 22 23 24 25 26 27 28 29 30 31

Jan Feb Mar Apr May Jun Jul Aug Sept Oct Nov Dec

1 2 3 4 5 6 7 8 9 10 11 12 13 14 15 16 17 18 19 20 21 22 23 24 25 26 27 28 29 30 31

Jan Feb Mar Apr May Jun Jul Aug Sept Oct Nov Dec

1 2 3 4 5 6 7 8 9 10 11 12 13 14 15 16 17 18 19 20 21 22 23 24 25
26 27 28 29 30 31

Jan Feb Mar Apr May Jun Jul Aug Sept Oct Nov Dec

1 2 3 4 5 6 7 8 9 10 11 12 13 14 15 16 17 18 19 20 21 22 23 24 25 26 27 28 29 30 31

'Worthy' refers to something or someone deserving of respect, attention, or consideration. It implies that the person or thing possesses qualities, achievements, or values that make them deserving of recognition or admiration. Being worthy suggests a sense of inherent value, worthiness, or merit. It can apply to various aspects of life, including personal character, accomplishments, contributions to society, or the significance of an idea or cause. So Lets get to worthy!

What does it mean to you to be worthy of love and care? How do you define your own worth and value as a person?

Jan Feb Mar Apr May Jun Jul Aug Sept Oct Nov Dec

1 2 3 4 5 6 7 8 9 10 11 12 13 14 15 16 17 18 19 20 21 22 23 24 25 26 27 28 29 30 31

Write about something that you admire about yourself. It could be a skill, a personality trait, or anything else that you feel proud of. How does this trait contribute to your sense of worth and value?

Jan Feb Mar Apr May Jun Jul Aug Sept Oct Nov Dec

1 2 3 4 5 6 7 8 9 10 11 12 13 14 15 16 17 18 19 20 21 22 23 24 25 26 27 28 29 30 31

Write a letter to yourself, expressing love and admiration for who you are as a person. List all of the qualities and traits that you admire about yourself, and reflect on how these qualities contribute to your sense of self-worth.

Dear,

Jan Feb Mar Apr May Jun Jul Aug Sept Oct Nov Dec

1 2 3 4 5 6 7 8 9 10 11 12 13 14 15 16 17 18 19 20 21 22 23 24 25 26 27 28 29 30 31

Jan Feb Mar Apr May Jun Jul Aug Sept Oct Nov Dec

1 2 3 4 5 6 7 8 9 10 11 12 13 14 15 16 17 18 19 20 21 22 23 24 25
26 27 28 29 30 31

Jan Feb Mar Apr May Jun Jul Aug Sept Oct Nov Dec

1 2 3 4 5 6 7 8 9 10 11 12 13 14 15 16 17 18 19 20 21 22 23 24 25 26 27 28 29 30 31

Jan Feb Mar Apr May Jun Jul Aug Sept Oct Nov Dec

1 2 3 4 5 6 7 8 9 10 11 12 13 14 15 16 17 18 19 20 21 22 23 24 25

26 27 28 29 30 31

Jan Feb Mar Apr May Jun Jul Aug Sept Oct Nov Dec

1 2 3 4 5 6 7 8 9 10 11 12 13 14 15 16 17 18 19 20 21 22 23 24 25
26 27 28 29 30 31

Jan Feb Mar Apr May Jun Jul Aug Sept Oct Nov Dec

1 2 3 4 5 6 7 8 9 10 11 12 13 14 15 16 17 18 19 20 21 22 23 24 25 26 27 28 29 30 31

Jan Feb Mar Apr May Jun Jul Aug Sept Oct Nov Dec

1 2 3 4 5 6 7 8 9 10 11 12 13 14 15 16 17 18 19 20 21 22 23 24 25
26 27 28 29 30 31

Jan Feb Mar Apr May Jun Jul Aug Sept Oct Nov Dec

1 2 3 4 5 6 7 8 9 10 11 12 13 14 15 16 17 18 19 20 21 22 23 24 25

26 27 28 29 30 31

Jan Feb Mar Apr May Jun Jul Aug Sept Oct Nov Dec

1 2 3 4 5 6 7 8 9 10 11 12 13 14 15 16 17 18 19 20 21 22 23 24 25 26 27 28 29 30 31

Jan Feb Mar Apr May Jun Jul Aug Sept Oct Nov Dec

1 2 3 4 5 6 7 8 9 10 11 12 13 14 15 16 17 18 19 20 21 22 23 24 25
26 27 28 29 30 31

Jan Feb Mar Apr May Jun Jul Aug Sept Oct Nov Dec

1 2 3 4 5 6 7 8 9 10 11 12 13 14 15 16 17 18 19 20 21 22 23 24 25 26 27 28 29 30 31

Jan Feb Mar Apr May Jun Jul Aug Sept Oct Nov Dec

1 2 3 4 5 6 7 8 9 10 11 12 13 14 15 16 17 18 19 20 21 22 23 24 25 26 27 28 29 30 31

Jan Feb Mar Apr May Jun Jul Aug Sept Oct Nov Dec

1 2 3 4 5 6 7 8 9 10 11 12 13 14 15 16 17 18 19 20 21 22 23 24 25 26 27 28 29 30 31

Jan Feb Mar Apr May Jun Jul Aug Sept Oct Nov Dec

1 2 3 4 5 6 7 8 9 10 11 12 13 14 15 16 17 18 19 20 21 22 23 24 25 26 27 28 29 30 31

Jan Feb Mar Apr May Jun Jul Aug Sept Oct Nov Dec

1 2 3 4 5 6 7 8 9 10 11 12 13 14 15 16 17 18 19 20 21 22 23 24 25 26 27 28 29 30 31

Jan Feb Mar Apr May Jun Jul Aug Sept Oct Nov Dec

1 2 3 4 5 6 7 8 9 10 11 12 13 14 15 16 17 18 19 20 21 22 23 24 25 26 27 28 29 30 31

Jan Feb Mar Apr May Jun Jul Aug Sept Oct Nov Dec

1 2 3 4 5 6 7 8 9 10 11 12 13 14 15 16 17 18 19 20 21 22 23 24 25 26 27 28 29 30 31

Jan Feb Mar Apr May Jun Jul Aug Sept Oct Nov Dec

1 2 3 4 5 6 7 8 9 10 11 12 13 14 15 16 17 18 19 20 21 22 23 24 25
26 27 28 29 30 31

Jan Feb Mar Apr May Jun Jul Aug Sept Oct Nov Dec

1 2 3 4 5 6 7 8 9 10 11 12 13 14 15 16 17 18 19 20 21 22 23 24 25 26 27 28 29 30 31

Jan Feb Mar Apr May Jun Jul Aug Sept Oct Nov Dec

1 2 3 4 5 6 7 8 9 10 11 12 13 14 15 16 17 18 19 20 21 22 23 24 25

26 27 28 29 30 31

Jan Feb Mar Apr May Jun Jul Aug Sept Oct Nov Dec

1 2 3 4 5 6 7 8 9 10 11 12 13 14 15 16 17 18 19 20 21 22 23 24 25

26 27 28 29 30 31

Jan Feb Mar Apr May Jun Jul Aug Sept Oct Nov Dec

1 2 3 4 5 6 7 8 9 10 11 12 13 14 15 16 17 18 19 20 21 22 23 24 25 26 27 28 29 30 31

Jan Feb Mar Apr May Jun Jul Aug Sept Oct Nov Dec

1 2 3 4 5 6 7 8 9 10 11 12 13 14 15 16 17 18 19 20 21 22 23 24 25 26 27 28 29 30 31

Jan Feb Mar Apr May Jun Jul Aug Sept Oct Nov Dec

1 2 3 4 5 6 7 8 9 10 11 12 13 14 15 16 17 18 19 20 21 22 23 24 25

26 27 28 29 30 31

Jan Feb Mar Apr May Jun Jul Aug Sept Oct Nov Dec

1 2 3 4 5 6 7 8 9 10 11 12 13 14 15 16 17 18 19 20 21 22 23 24 25

26 27 28 29 30 31

Jan Feb Mar Apr May Jun Jul Aug Sept Oct Nov Dec

1 2 3 4 5 6 7 8 9 10 11 12 13 14 15 16 17 18 19 20 21 22 23 24 25

26 27 28 29 30 31

Jan Feb Mar Apr May Jun Jul Aug Sept Oct Nov Dec

1 2 3 4 5 6 7 8 9 10 11 12 13 14 15 16 17 18 19 20 21 22 23 24 25

26 27 28 29 30 31

Jan Feb Mar Apr May Jun Jul Aug Sept Oct Nov Dec

1 2 3 4 5 6 7 8 9 10 11 12 13 14 15 16 17 18 19 20 21 22 23 24 25

26 27 28 29 30 31

Jan Feb Mar Apr May Jun Jul Aug Sept Oct Nov Dec

1 2 3 4 5 6 7 8 9 10 11 12 13 14 15 16 17 18 19 20 21 22 23 24 25
26 27 28 29 30 31

Jan Feb Mar Apr May Jun Jul Aug Sept Oct Nov Dec

1 2 3 4 5 6 7 8 9 10 11 12 13 14 15 16 17 18 19 20 21 22 23 24 25

26 27 28 29 30 31

Jan Feb Mar Apr May Jun Jul Aug Sept Oct Nov Dec

1 2 3 4 5 6 7 8 9 10 11 12 13 14 15 16 17 18 19 20 21 22 23 24 25 26 27 28 29 30 31

Jan Feb Mar Apr May Jun Jul Aug Sept Oct Nov Dec

1 2 3 4 5 6 7 8 9 10 11 12 13 14 15 16 17 18 19 20 21 22 23 24 25

26 27 28 29 30 31

Jan Feb Mar Apr May Jun Jul Aug Sept Oct Nov Dec

1 2 3 4 5 6 7 8 9 10 11 12 13 14 15 16 17 18 19 20 21 22 23 24 25
26 27 28 29 30 31

Jan Feb Mar Apr May Jun Jul Aug Sept Oct Nov Dec

1 2 3 4 5 6 7 8 9 10 11 12 13 14 15 16 17 18 19 20 21 22 23 24 25

26 27 28 29 30 31

Jan Feb Mar Apr May Jun Jul Aug Sept Oct Nov Dec

1 2 3 4 5 6 7 8 9 10 11 12 13 14 15 16 17 18 19 20 21 22 23 24 25
26 27 28 29 30 31

Jan Feb Mar Apr May Jun Jul Aug Sept Oct Nov Dec

1 2 3 4 5 6 7 8 9 10 11 12 13 14 15 16 17 18 19 20 21 22 23 24 25 26 27 28 29 30 31

Jan Feb Mar Apr May Jun Jul Aug Sept Oct Nov Dec

1 2 3 4 5 6 7 8 9 10 11 12 13 14 15 16 17 18 19 20 21 22 23 24 25
26 27 28 29 30 31

Jan Feb Mar Apr May Jun Jul Aug Sept Oct Nov Dec

1 2 3 4 5 6 7 8 9 10 11 12 13 14 15 16 17 18 19 20 21 22 23 24 25
26 27 28 29 30 31

Jan Feb Mar Apr May Jun Jul Aug Sept Oct Nov Dec

1 2 3 4 5 6 7 8 9 10 11 12 13 14 15 16 17 18 19 20 21 22 23 24 25 26 27 28 29 30 31

Jan Feb Mar Apr May Jun Jul Aug Sept Oct Nov Dec

1 2 3 4 5 6 7 8 9 10 11 12 13 14 15 16 17 18 19 20 21 22 23 24 25

26 27 28 29 30 31

Jan Feb Mar Apr May Jun Jul Aug Sept Oct Nov Dec

1 2 3 4 5 6 7 8 9 10 11 12 13 14 15 16 17 18 19 20 21 22 23 24 25 26 27 28 29 30 31

Jan Feb Mar Apr May Jun Jul Aug Sept Oct Nov Dec

1 2 3 4 5 6 7 8 9 10 11 12 13 14 15 16 17 18 19 20 21 22 23 24 25
26 27 28 29 30 31

Jan Feb Mar Apr May Jun Jul Aug Sept Oct Nov Dec

1 2 3 4 5 6 7 8 9 10 11 12 13 14 15 16 17 18 19 20 21 22 23 24 25
26 27 28 29 30 31

Jan Feb Mar Apr May Jun Jul Aug Sept Oct Nov Dec

1 2 3 4 5 6 7 8 9 10 11 12 13 14 15 16 17 18 19 20 21 22 23 24 25
26 27 28 29 30 31

Jan Feb Mar Apr May Jun Jul Aug Sept Oct Nov Dec

1 2 3 4 5 6 7 8 9 10 11 12 13 14 15 16 17 18 19 20 21 22 23 24 25

26 27 28 29 30 31

Jan Feb Mar Apr May Jun Jul Aug Sept Oct Nov Dec

1 2 3 4 5 6 7 8 9 10 11 12 13 14 15 16 17 18 19 20 21 22 23 24 25
26 27 28 29 30 31

Jan Feb Mar Apr May Jun Jul Aug Sept Oct Nov Dec

1 2 3 4 5 6 7 8 9 10 11 12 13 14 15 16 17 18 19 20 21 22 23 24 25 26 27 28 29 30 31

Jan Feb Mar Apr May Jun Jul Aug Sept Oct Nov Dec

1 2 3 4 5 6 7 8 9 10 11 12 13 14 15 16 17 18 19 20 21 22 23 24 25
26 27 28 29 30 31

Jan Feb Mar Apr May Jun Jul Aug Sept Oct Nov Dec

1 2 3 4 5 6 7 8 9 10 11 12 13 14 15 16 17 18 19 20 21 22 23 24 25 26 27 28 29 30 31

Jan Feb Mar Apr May Jun Jul Aug Sept Oct Nov Dec

1 2 3 4 5 6 7 8 9 10 11 12 13 14 15 16 17 18 19 20 21 22 23 24 25
26 27 28 29 30 31

Jan Feb Mar Apr May Jun Jul Aug Sept Oct Nov Dec

1 2 3 4 5 6 7 8 9 10 11 12 13 14 15 16 17 18 19 20 21 22 23 24 25

26 27 28 29 30 31

Jan Feb Mar Apr May Jun Jul Aug Sept Oct Nov Dec

1 2 3 4 5 6 7 8 9 10 11 12 13 14 15 16 17 18 19 20 21 22 23 24 25
26 27 28 29 30 31

Jan Feb Mar Apr May Jun Jul Aug Sept Oct Nov Dec

1 2 3 4 5 6 7 8 9 10 11 12 13 14 15 16 17 18 19 20 21 22 23 24 25

26 27 28 29 30 31

Jan Feb Mar Apr May Jun Jul Aug Sept Oct Nov Dec

1 2 3 4 5 6 7 8 9 10 11 12 13 14 15 16 17 18 19 20 21 22 23 24 25 26 27 28 29 30 31

Jan Feb Mar Apr May Jun Jul Aug Sept Oct Nov Dec

1 2 3 4 5 6 7 8 9 10 11 12 13 14 15 16 17 18 19 20 21 22 23 24 25
26 27 28 29 30 31

Jan Feb Mar Apr May Jun Jul Aug Sept Oct Nov Dec

1 2 3 4 5 6 7 8 9 10 11 12 13 14 15 16 17 18 19 20 21 22 23 24 25

26 27 28 29 30 31

Jan Feb Mar Apr May Jun Jul Aug Sept Oct Nov Dec

1 2 3 4 5 6 7 8 9 10 11 12 13 14 15 16 17 18 19 20 21 22 23 24 25 26 27 28 29 30 31

Jan Feb Mar Apr May Jun Jul Aug Sept Oct Nov Dec

1 2 3 4 5 6 7 8 9 10 11 12 13 14 15 16 17 18 19 20 21 22 23 24 25

26 27 28 29 30 31

Jan Feb Mar Apr May Jun Jul Aug Sept Oct Nov Dec

1 2 3 4 5 6 7 8 9 10 11 12 13 14 15 16 17 18 19 20 21 22 23 24 25
26 27 28 29 30 31

Jan Feb Mar Apr May Jun Jul Aug Sept Oct Nov Dec

1 2 3 4 5 6 7 8 9 10 11 12 13 14 15 16 17 18 19 20 21 22 23 24 25

26 27 28 29 30 31

Jan Feb Mar Apr May Jun Jul Aug Sept Oct Nov Dec

1 2 3 4 5 6 7 8 9 10 11 12 13 14 15 16 17 18 19 20 21 22 23 24 25 26 27 28 29 30 31

Jan Feb Mar Apr May Jun Jul Aug Sept Oct Nov Dec

1 2 3 4 5 6 7 8 9 10 11 12 13 14 15 16 17 18 19 20 21 22 23 24 25

26 27 28 29 30 31

Jan Feb Mar Apr May Jun Jul Aug Sept Oct Nov Dec

1 2 3 4 5 6 7 8 9 10 11 12 13 14 15 16 17 18 19 20 21 22 23 24 25
26 27 28 29 30 31

Jan Feb Mar Apr May Jun Jul Aug Sept Oct Nov Dec

1 2 3 4 5 6 7 8 9 10 11 12 13 14 15 16 17 18 19 20 21 22 23 24 25 26 27 28 29 30 31

Jan Feb Mar Apr May Jun Jul Aug Sept Oct Nov Dec

1 2 3 4 5 6 7 8 9 10 11 12 13 14 15 16 17 18 19 20 21 22 23 24 25
26 27 28 29 30 31

Jan Feb Mar Apr May Jun Jul Aug Sept Oct Nov Dec

1 2 3 4 5 6 7 8 9 10 11 12 13 14 15 16 17 18 19 20 21 22 23 24 25

26 27 28 29 30 31

Jan Feb Mar Apr May Jun Jul Aug Sept Oct Nov Dec

1 2 3 4 5 6 7 8 9 10 11 12 13 14 15 16 17 18 19 20 21 22 23 24 25
26 27 28 29 30 31

Jan Feb Mar Apr May Jun Jul Aug Sept Oct Nov Dec

1 2 3 4 5 6 7 8 9 10 11 12 13 14 15 16 17 18 19 20 21 22 23 24 25

26 27 28 29 30 31

Jan Feb Mar Apr May Jun Jul Aug Sept Oct Nov Dec

1 2 3 4 5 6 7 8 9 10 11 12 13 14 15 16 17 18 19 20 21 22 23 24 25
26 27 28 29 30 31

Jan Feb Mar Apr May Jun Jul Aug Sept Oct Nov Dec

1 2 3 4 5 6 7 8 9 10 11 12 13 14 15 16 17 18 19 20 21 22 23 24 25 26 27 28 29 30 31

Write a list of affirmations that reinforce your sense of worth and value as a person. Read these affirmations aloud to yourself every day, and allow them to sink in and become a part of your daily practice of self-love.

Jan Feb Mar Apr May Jun Jul Aug Sept Oct Nov Dec

1 2 3 4 5 6 7 8 9 10 11 12 13 14 15 16 17 18 19 20 21 22 23 24 25
26 27 28 29 30 31

Jan Feb Mar Apr May Jun Jul Aug Sept Oct Nov Dec

1 2 3 4 5 6 7 8 9 10 11 12 13 14 15 16 17 18 19 20 21 22 23 24 25 26 27 28 29 30 31

Jan Feb Mar Apr May Jun Jul Aug Sept Oct Nov Dec

1 2 3 4 5 6 7 8 9 10 11 12 13 14 15 16 17 18 19 20 21 22 23 24 25

26 27 28 29 30 31

Jan Feb Mar Apr May Jun Jul Aug Sept Oct Nov Dec

1 2 3 4 5 6 7 8 9 10 11 12 13 14 15 16 17 18 19 20 21 22 23 24 25 26 27 28 29 30 31

Jan Feb Mar Apr May Jun Jul Aug Sept Oct Nov Dec

1 2 3 4 5 6 7 8 9 10 11 12 13 14 15 16 17 18 19 20 21 22 23 24 25 26 27 28 29 30 31

Jan Feb Mar Apr May Jun Jul Aug Sept Oct Nov Dec

1 2 3 4 5 6 7 8 9 10 11 12 13 14 15 16 17 18 19 20 21 22 23 24 25

26 27 28 29 30 31

Jan Feb Mar Apr May Jun Jul Aug Sept Oct Nov Dec

1 2 3 4 5 6 7 8 9 10 11 12 13 14 15 16 17 18 19 20 21 22 23 24 25

26 27 28 29 30 31

Jan Feb Mar Apr May Jun Jul Aug Sept Oct Nov Dec

1 2 3 4 5 6 7 8 9 10 11 12 13 14 15 16 17 18 19 20 21 22 23 24 25 26 27 28 29 30 31

Jan Feb Mar Apr May Jun Jul Aug Sept Oct Nov Dec

1 2 3 4 5 6 7 8 9 10 11 12 13 14 15 16 17 18 19 20 21 22 23 24 25

26 27 28 29 30 31

Jan Feb Mar Apr May Jun Jul Aug Sept Oct Nov Dec

1 2 3 4 5 6 7 8 9 10 11 12 13 14 15 16 17 18 19 20 21 22 23 24 25 26 27 28 29 30 31

Jan Feb Mar Apr May Jun Jul Aug Sept Oct Nov Dec

1 2 3 4 5 6 7 8 9 10 11 12 13 14 15 16 17 18 19 20 21 22 23 24 25 26 27 28 29 30 31

Jan Feb Mar Apr May Jun Jul Aug Sept Oct Nov Dec

1 2 3 4 5 6 7 8 9 10 11 12 13 14 15 16 17 18 19 20 21 22 23 24 25

26 27 28 29 30 31

Jan Feb Mar Apr May Jun Jul Aug Sept Oct Nov Dec

1 2 3 4 5 6 7 8 9 10 11 12 13 14 15 16 17 18 19 20 21 22 23 24 25
26 27 28 29 30 31

Jan Feb Mar Apr May Jun Jul Aug Sept Oct Nov Dec

1 2 3 4 5 6 7 8 9 10 11 12 13 14 15 16 17 18 19 20 21 22 23 24 25
26 27 28 29 30 31

Jan Feb Mar Apr May Jun Jul Aug Sept Oct Nov Dec

1 2 3 4 5 6 7 8 9 10 11 12 13 14 15 16 17 18 19 20 21 22 23 24 25 26 27 28 29 30 31

Jan Feb Mar Apr May Jun Jul Aug Sept Oct Nov Dec

1 2 3 4 5 6 7 8 9 10 11 12 13 14 15 16 17 18 19 20 21 22 23 24 25

26 27 28 29 30 31

Jan Feb Mar Apr May Jun Jul Aug Sept Oct Nov Dec

1 2 3 4 5 6 7 8 9 10 11 12 13 14 15 16 17 18 19 20 21 22 23 24 25
26 27 28 29 30 31

Jan Feb Mar Apr May Jun Jul Aug Sept Oct Nov Dec

1 2 3 4 5 6 7 8 9 10 11 12 13 14 15 16 17 18 19 20 21 22 23 24 25
26 27 28 29 30 31

Jan Feb Mar Apr May Jun Jul Aug Sept Oct Nov Dec

1 2 3 4 5 6 7 8 9 10 11 12 13 14 15 16 17 18 19 20 21 22 23 24 25

26 27 28 29 30 31

Jan Feb Mar Apr May Jun Jul Aug Sept Oct Nov Dec

1 2 3 4 5 6 7 8 9 10 11 12 13 14 15 16 17 18 19 20 21 22 23 24 25

26 27 28 29 30 31

Jan Feb Mar Apr May Jun Jul Aug Sept Oct Nov Dec

1 2 3 4 5 6 7 8 9 10 11 12 13 14 15 16 17 18 19 20 21 22 23 24 25
26 27 28 29 30 31

Jan Feb Mar Apr May Jun Jul Aug Sept Oct Nov Dec

1 2 3 4 5 6 7 8 9 10 11 12 13 14 15 16 17 18 19 20 21 22 23 24 25 26 27 28 29 30 31

Jan Feb Mar Apr May Jun Jul Aug Sept Oct Nov Dec

1 2 3 4 5 6 7 8 9 10 11 12 13 14 15 16 17 18 19 20 21 22 23 24 25 26 27 28 29 30 31

Jan Feb Mar Apr May Jun Jul Aug Sept Oct Nov Dec

1 2 3 4 5 6 7 8 9 10 11 12 13 14 15 16 17 18 19 20 21 22 23 24 25 26 27 28 29 30 31

Jan Feb Mar Apr May Jun Jul Aug Sept Oct Nov Dec

1 2 3 4 5 6 7 8 9 10 11 12 13 14 15 16 17 18 19 20 21 22 23 24 25 26 27 28 29 30 31

Jan Feb Mar Apr May Jun Jul Aug Sept Oct Nov Dec

1 2 3 4 5 6 7 8 9 10 11 12 13 14 15 16 17 18 19 20 21 22 23 24 25
26 27 28 29 30 31

Jan Feb Mar Apr May Jun Jul Aug Sept Oct Nov Dec

1 2 3 4 5 6 7 8 9 10 11 12 13 14 15 16 17 18 19 20 21 22 23 24 25 26 27 28 29 30 31

Jan Feb Mar Apr May Jun Jul Aug Sept Oct Nov Dec

1 2 3 4 5 6 7 8 9 10 11 12 13 14 15 16 17 18 19 20 21 22 23 24 25 26 27 28 29 30 31

Jan Feb Mar Apr May Jun Jul Aug Sept Oct Nov Dec

1 2 3 4 5 6 7 8 9 10 11 12 13 14 15 16 17 18 19 20 21 22 23 24 25

26 27 28 29 30 31

Jan Feb Mar Apr May Jun Jul Aug Sept Oct Nov Dec

1 2 3 4 5 6 7 8 9 10 11 12 13 14 15 16 17 18 19 20 21 22 23 24 25
26 27 28 29 30 31

Jan Feb Mar Apr May Jun Jul Aug Sept Oct Nov Dec

1 2 3 4 5 6 7 8 9 10 11 12 13 14 15 16 17 18 19 20 21 22 23 24 25 26 27 28 29 30 31

Jan Feb Mar Apr May Jun Jul Aug Sept Oct Nov Dec

1 2 3 4 5 6 7 8 9 10 11 12 13 14 15 16 17 18 19 20 21 22 23 24 25
26 27 28 29 30 31

Jan Feb Mar Apr May Jun Jul Aug Sept Oct Nov Dec

1 2 3 4 5 6 7 8 9 10 11 12 13 14 15 16 17 18 19 20 21 22 23 24 25 26 27 28 29 30 31

Jan Feb Mar Apr May Jun Jul Aug Sept Oct Nov Dec

1 2 3 4 5 6 7 8 9 10 11 12 13 14 15 16 17 18 19 20 21 22 23 24 25 26 27 28 29 30 31

Jan Feb Mar Apr May Jun Jul Aug Sept Oct Nov Dec

1 2 3 4 5 6 7 8 9 10 11 12 13 14 15 16 17 18 19 20 21 22 23 24 25
26 27 28 29 30 31

Jan Feb Mar Apr May Jun Jul Aug Sept Oct Nov Dec

1 2 3 4 5 6 7 8 9 10 11 12 13 14 15 16 17 18 19 20 21 22 23 24 25
26 27 28 29 30 31

Jan Feb Mar Apr May Jun Jul Aug Sept Oct Nov Dec

1 2 3 4 5 6 7 8 9 10 11 12 13 14 15 16 17 18 19 20 21 22 23 24 25

26 27 28 29 30 31

Jan Feb Mar Apr May Jun Jul Aug Sept Oct Nov Dec

1 2 3 4 5 6 7 8 9 10 11 12 13 14 15 16 17 18 19 20 21 22 23 24 25 26 27 28 29 30 31

Jan Feb Mar Apr May Jun Jul Aug Sept Oct Nov Dec

1 2 3 4 5 6 7 8 9 10 11 12 13 14 15 16 17 18 19 20 21 22 23 24 25 26 27 28 29 30 31

Jan Feb Mar Apr May Jun Jul Aug Sept Oct Nov Dec

1 2 3 4 5 6 7 8 9 10 11 12 13 14 15 16 17 18 19 20 21 22 23 24 25

26 27 28 29 30 31

Jan Feb Mar Apr May Jun Jul Aug Sept Oct Nov Dec

1 2 3 4 5 6 7 8 9 10 11 12 13 14 15 16 17 18 19 20 21 22 23 24 25
26 27 28 29 30 31

Jan Feb Mar Apr May Jun Jul Aug Sept Oct Nov Dec

1 2 3 4 5 6 7 8 9 10 11 12 13 14 15 16 17 18 19 20 21 22 23 24 25 26 27 28 29 30 31

Jan Feb Mar Apr May Jun Jul Aug Sept Oct Nov Dec

1 2 3 4 5 6 7 8 9 10 11 12 13 14 15 16 17 18 19 20 21 22 23 24 25 26 27 28 29 30 31

Jan Feb Mar Apr May Jun Jul Aug Sept Oct Nov Dec

1 2 3 4 5 6 7 8 9 10 11 12 13 14 15 16 17 18 19 20 21 22 23 24 25

26 27 28 29 30 31

Jan Feb Mar Apr May Jun Jul Aug Sept Oct Nov Dec

1 2 3 4 5 6 7 8 9 10 11 12 13 14 15 16 17 18 19 20 21 22 23 24 25 26 27 28 29 30 31

Jan Feb Mar Apr May Jun Jul Aug Sept Oct Nov Dec

1 2 3 4 5 6 7 8 9 10 11 12 13 14 15 16 17 18 19 20 21 22 23 24 25

26 27 28 29 30 31

Jan Feb Mar Apr May Jun Jul Aug Sept Oct Nov Dec

1 2 3 4 5 6 7 8 9 10 11 12 13 14 15 16 17 18 19 20 21 22 23 24 25

26 27 28 29 30 31

Jan Feb Mar Apr May Jun Jul Aug Sept Oct Nov Dec

1 2 3 4 5 6 7 8 9 10 11 12 13 14 15 16 17 18 19 20 21 22 23 24 25

26 27 28 29 30 31

Jan Feb Mar Apr May Jun Jul Aug Sept Oct Nov Dec

1 2 3 4 5 6 7 8 9 10 11 12 13 14 15 16 17 18 19 20 21 22 23 24 25 26 27 28 29 30 31

Jan Feb Mar Apr May Jun Jul Aug Sept Oct Nov Dec

1 2 3 4 5 6 7 8 9 10 11 12 13 14 15 16 17 18 19 20 21 22 23 24 25 26 27 28 29 30 31

Jan Feb Mar Apr May Jun Jul Aug Sept Oct Nov Dec

1 2 3 4 5 6 7 8 9 10 11 12 13 14 15 16 17 18 19 20 21 22 23 24 25
26 27 28 29 30 31

Jan Feb Mar Apr May Jun Jul Aug Sept Oct Nov Dec

1 2 3 4 5 6 7 8 9 10 11 12 13 14 15 16 17 18 19 20 21 22 23 24 25 26 27 28 29 30 31

Jan Feb Mar Apr May Jun Jul Aug Sept Oct Nov Dec

1 2 3 4 5 6 7 8 9 10 11 12 13 14 15 16 17 18 19 20 21 22 23 24 25 26 27 28 29 30 31

Jan Feb Mar Apr May Jun Jul Aug Sept Oct Nov Dec

1 2 3 4 5 6 7 8 9 10 11 12 13 14 15 16 17 18 19 20 21 22 23 24 25

26 27 28 29 30 31

Jan Feb Mar Apr May Jun Jul Aug Sept Oct Nov Dec

1 2 3 4 5 6 7 8 9 10 11 12 13 14 15 16 17 18 19 20 21 22 23 24 25 26 27 28 29 30 31

Jan Feb Mar Apr May Jun Jul Aug Sept Oct Nov Dec

1 2 3 4 5 6 7 8 9 10 11 12 13 14 15 16 17 18 19 20 21 22 23 24 25

26 27 28 29 30 31

Jan Feb Mar Apr May Jun Jul Aug Sept Oct Nov Dec

1 2 3 4 5 6 7 8 9 10 11 12 13 14 15 16 17 18 19 20 21 22 23 24 25 26 27 28 29 30 31

Jan Feb Mar Apr May Jun Jul Aug Sept Oct Nov Dec

1 2 3 4 5 6 7 8 9 10 11 12 13 14 15 16 17 18 19 20 21 22 23 24 25
26 27 28 29 30 31

Jan Feb Mar Apr May Jun Jul Aug Sept Oct Nov Dec

1 2 3 4 5 6 7 8 9 10 11 12 13 14 15 16 17 18 19 20 21 22 23 24 25 26 27 28 29 30 31

Jan Feb Mar Apr May Jun Jul Aug Sept Oct Nov Dec

1 2 3 4 5 6 7 8 9 10 11 12 13 14 15 16 17 18 19 20 21 22 23 24 25
26 27 28 29 30 31

Jan Feb Mar Apr May Jun Jul Aug Sept Oct Nov Dec

1 2 3 4 5 6 7 8 9 10 11 12 13 14 15 16 17 18 19 20 21 22 23 24 25

26 27 28 29 30 31

Jan Feb Mar Apr May Jun Jul Aug Sept Oct Nov Dec

1 2 3 4 5 6 7 8 9 10 11 12 13 14 15 16 17 18 19 20 21 22 23 24 25 26 27 28 29 30 31

Jan Feb Mar Apr May Jun Jul Aug Sept Oct Nov Dec

1 2 3 4 5 6 7 8 9 10 11 12 13 14 15 16 17 18 19 20 21 22 23 24 25 26 27 28 29 30 31

Jan Feb Mar Apr May Jun Jul Aug Sept Oct Nov Dec

1 2 3 4 5 6 7 8 9 10 11 12 13 14 15 16 17 18 19 20 21 22 23 24 25 26 27 28 29 30 31

Jan Feb Mar Apr May Jun Jul Aug Sept Oct Nov Dec

1 2 3 4 5 6 7 8 9 10 11 12 13 14 15 16 17 18 19 20 21 22 23 24 25 26 27 28 29 30 31

Jan Feb Mar Apr May Jun Jul Aug Sept Oct Nov Dec

1 2 3 4 5 6 7 8 9 10 11 12 13 14 15 16 17 18 19 20 21 22 23 24 25
26 27 28 29 30 31

Jan Feb Mar Apr May Jun Jul Aug Sept Oct Nov Dec

1 2 3 4 5 6 7 8 9 10 11 12 13 14 15 16 17 18 19 20 21 22 23 24 25 26 27 28 29 30 31

Jan Feb Mar Apr May Jun Jul Aug Sept Oct Nov Dec

1 2 3 4 5 6 7 8 9 10 11 12 13 14 15 16 17 18 19 20 21 22 23 24 25

26 27 28 29 30 31

Jan Feb Mar Apr May Jun Jul Aug Sept Oct Nov Dec

1 2 3 4 5 6 7 8 9 10 11 12 13 14 15 16 17 18 19 20 21 22 23 24 25 26 27 28 29 30 31

Jan Feb Mar Apr May Jun Jul Aug Sept Oct Nov Dec

1 2 3 4 5 6 7 8 9 10 11 12 13 14 15 16 17 18 19 20 21 22 23 24 25 26 27 28 29 30 31

Stop and repeat after me "I love myself because__"

Made in the USA
Columbia, SC
11 April 2024

34175705R00148